Euphemisms

Softer Answers
to Grievous Questions

or

Name-calling Solves Nothing

... and other miscellaneous thoughts

Rob Woodfin

Parson's Porch Books
www.parsonsporchbooks.com

Euphemisms

978-1-949888-97-3

ISBN: Softcover

Euphemisms

Contents

Underwood

Preface

I grew up watching my dad write news and editorials for The South Pittsburg Hustler on the same Underwood typewriter his dad had used. With his two index fingers he seemed almost as fast as the typesetters back in the shop who were using all of theirs.

Like myself, Dad had no formal training in journalism, but also like myself he graduated from a master class taught by his dad.

My mother taught me to love to read.
My dad taught me to love to write.

And I still do.

Our flag salutes free speech

There is so much bombast recently vilifying people who protest inequities of one kind or another which happen in the shadow of our flag. When injustices are sanctioned by principalities and powers, or simply ignored by those in authority, the flag sometimes becomes the focus of the protest ... especially when the principals in charge have wrapped themselves in the flag and belligerently refused to listen. It is not our honored dead who lie under the flags at Arlington that protestors are challenging, it is the arrogant abusers of power in the gated fortresses under the flags at either end of Pennsylvania Avenue. And who among us doesn't honestly understand that?

I never wore the uniform. I registered for the draft, but they stopped calling numbers before they got to mine. I surely appreciate and respect our service men and women, and I don't pretend to speak for them. I certainly did not earn the empathy to speak for those who died. But I wonder, did any of them die for the flag? I know they died under the flag ... with the flag ... showing allegiance to the flag. But I've always assumed it was their neighbors around the flag that they gave their lives to protect.

Christ didn't die for the Jewish flag ... nor the Christian flag ... nor for any symbol ... not even the cross. He died for humanity. When we castigate those who protest injustices in the world and put more value on symbols than people, we devalue humanity.

It is certainly your right to disagree with people who are protesting. But loving symbols more than people is offensive ... not to me ... none of my business who you love or hate. I sincerely believe, however, that loving symbols more than children of God, no matter how disagreeable you may consider them, is offensive to God.

We have not become so polarized, so divisive, so angry by chance. Our brokenness is by design ... carefully, skillfully, methodically brought about by those who benefit from our divides; not those in uniform, not those on the assembly line, but those you and I never see; those whose only interest in the flag is how it can be used to bolster their enormous wealth and power.

Our flag is never more desecrated than when it is used by aspiring plutocrats to usurp the republic for which it stands.

20190716

Similar but Not the Same

Yes, what's happening in Venezuela could one day soon happen here. But not for the reasons being blurted by the facsimiles of Roger Ailes. Democratic socialism, which we've practiced for nearly a century in the United States, is not why our South American neighbor is in such a shamble. We do, however, share dangerous traits in common.

Socialism has many forms, and it is not hard to find bad examples.

Usually the examples you hear are of dictatorial regimes which camouflage themselves under some type of socialist system. Our experiment followed a different pattern and likely helped us avoid revolution in the 1930s leading to an outcome like the Soviet Union. Even those who disparage FDR will admit that people rarely starve to death en masse voluntarily.

The New Deal arrested starvation in this country during the Great Depression and laid the groundwork for the economic pinnacle to which we rose in the 1950s/60s.

Venezuela's condition is not because their government is spending all its money on the poor. It is failing for two primary reasons: hyperinflation due to exploding debt and extreme wealth disparity following years of ravenous dictatorial rule.

Our record deficits (which some talking heads are now actually trying to claim don't matter) are primarily because of record tax rollbacks, which may spill down to some below the billionaire class at the moment but won't be fondly remembered by anyone except the 1% should (when) hyperinflation occurs here.

Venezuela should be an alarm bell for us. But not because of our history of taking care of the less fortunate or taxing people and companies based on how well they are doing and using the proceeds to build a better America. The bell is tolling for us due to the unfettered greed at the top of the food chain ... in North and South America. The lesson all nations have to relearn again and again: avarice doesn't salute flags, it corrupts them.

20190720

Great for Whom?

Asterism. Good word. Look it up. I did. The definition is "subtle mockery." An example of it is a backhanded compliment. Maybe a better example is "Make America Great Again."

Who thinks it isn't? But the better question: who is excluded from the greatness of America? Who has been in the past? Who will continue to be, despite our rhetoric?

America has always been great ... even before the Constitution said so ... for some. But there have also always been exceptions and exclusions. The word "equal" may have flowed from Jefferson's pen, but the application from the outset has never fully, truly been.

Protesting this inequality is okay, so long as you are quiet about it and do it in some dark, insulated closet. But make anyone uncomfortable by coming out of the closet and you are labeled a troublemaker, an America-hater, an undesirable; "the problem."

Megan Rapinoe, captain of the National Women's Soccer League that just won the World Cup, says it is time for a reckoning about the exclusion of so many from the greatness enjoyed by such a select few ... an elite few which becomes fewer with each passing year, by the way. Her interviews this week have outraged some. of course. But she is spot on and is using this moment in the spotlight very effectively.

We don't need an ever smaller select group anointed as eligible for the greatness of America. What we need is a bigger hat. It should read, "Let's finally make America great for everybody, no matter how meager their resources, no matter what color they are, no matter who they love."
That should be our goal. A win/win/win. At long last.

20190711

Imperfection ≠ Malfeasance

I just finished Jon Meacham's book on Thomas Jefferson, *The Art of Power.* The biggest take-away for me was not how great he became, but how imperfect he was. And yet he processed beyond his many flaws to do great things, to make enormous contributions to causes he held dear and we still revere today.

What we may be doing at this moment in history is over-reacting to any mistake someone has ever made. Insisting on perfection, knowing full well it doesn't exist. And perhaps that creates a counterweight effect in our culture that throws up its hands and accepts the antithesis to propriety, so long as their own immediate itch is scratched.

Putting people on pedestals is risky business. But tearing down every potential leader before they can even get their toe in the water is costlier by far.

20190705

Gerrymandering

Gerrymandering is what incumbent Congressmen and Senators do to pick their voters. And each passing year we the people cede just a little more control of how our country is run. At the moment this abdication favors enough citizens whose agendas are being served that the status quid-pro-quo is safely ensconced. But in the not-too-distant future those agendas won't matter anymore because plutocracy will be firmly in place and elections merely an artifice. The Supreme ruling today testifies to this trajectory.

The surest part of this tragedy is that the working class will endure, as they always have, because they are tough enough to make do no matter how dire the circumstance. The ironic part regards the affluent enablers whose progeny will one day wake up to find that the government is no longer returning their lobbyists' phone calls. Aristocracy needs not abide anyone below their class, including bourgeoisie billionaires.

One more certainty: oligarchs never acquire governments with humanitarian intentions.

20190627

Hard to Unremember

A recent article about children of Nazi leaders, soldiers and supporters in post-World War II Germany is especially chilling in the context of recent activities in our own country. Be adamantly opposed to immigration in whichever forms you choose, that is your legitimate option. But choose to support the program of child detention centers at your own peril. You might earnestly excuse yourself. God may even forgive you. But it could be a different story with your children and your grandchildren once we recover from our present circumstance, our strong delusion that anything we do as Americans is right because Americans can never be wrong.

Some German children spent the rest of their lives trying to repair their parents' reputations. Others shunned any discussion or memory of their previous generation, wanting nothing to do with the atrocities that would haunt them, nonetheless.

For a while I also thought this comparison might be too extreme, not strictly applicable. But as we watch officials testify in attempts to justify these facilities, and as we learn details of the enterprises making substantial profits from a program repugnant on its face and abhorrent in its conditions, it is derelict to remain passive ... and untenable to remain intentionally ignorant.

At least one resistance leader has used the term concentration camps and is being excoriated for it. And yet we have extremist examples of officials this month mounting platforms and podiums not far from us calling for the extermination of undesirables in our midst. One thing does lead to another ... at least when a silent majority makes it possible.

There is a fail-safe point beyond the rule of law. And once we fly past it ... yes, we ... only the people with the golden parachutes will be able to enjoy a happy landing.

20190625

City Life

I drove past city hall this morning to see if it was surrounded by county and state police. It appears alleged illegal activities were heavy on the alleged and somewhat trumped up on the illegal. I did see city crews out dealing with the effects of last night's storm, and so "business as usual" seemed to be the more accurate assessment of the City of South Pittsburg and its long history of overcoming adversity to remain the beautiful, big-hearted small town most of us love to live in, be from and brag about.

I know what it's like to be frustrated, to have suggestions ignored and people seemingly standing in line to disagree with every thought, word and deed. It is disheartening. But most of us who have reached the edge of old age and still keep trying every day have come to realize that sometimes we have been wrong and were fortunate to be surrounded by folks willing to keep us on the right track.

There are citizens who call the TV news to come to South Pittsburg every time they think something needs to get investigated. And I tend to agree that a little bit of paranoia can be a healthy thing, because every great once in a while somebody really could be out to get you. Perhaps the better part of valor in this case, though, would be to just show up at a city meeting and listen sometime. Don't come to rant or expect to see people lining their pockets with your money. Come and watch a group of people who love this city as much as you do putting forth the effort to make it a little bit better. You might just come away realizing this ain't such a bad place to call home.

20190620

Collateral Sins

"The collateral sins of our culture." I heard those words Sunday morning and it reminded me of hearing a sonic boom.

What was that!?!

The context was "rarely do we reflect on the collateral sins of our culture." The greater context was an excellent Pentecost sermon reminding us that joy and peace are not out of our reach this side of eternity ... if we find the courage to stop building barriers between "us and them" and use our collective strength to build the community we long for ... with God's help.

How Pentecostal is that?

So often we find ourselves wishing that "they" wouldn't do things that put our health and safety at risk or adversely affect our economy or, or, or. But when those thoughts occur to us, we might pick up a dictionary and remind ourselves how to spell, pronounce and define "disingenuous." The theys out there can only do what they do as long as we sit passively at the spiritual bus stop waiting to get our ticket punched. Where we belong is out there on the street using our gifts to honor the creation we've been blessed with.

In the Episcopal Church, we routinely ask forgiveness for sinful things we have done ... AND ... what we have left undone. And in that confession, we all take ownership of the collateral sins of our culture.

Boom.

20190611

Twisted

Halfway between Birmingham and the Mississippi state line on I-22 lies the town of Carbon Hill, Alabama. Roughly the size of South Pittsburg, it was also established about the same time, faced similar economic setbacks, was bolstered by the WPA (rather than TVA) after the Great Depression, and continues today as a small, quiet, average Southern town.

Perhaps the biggest difference between that community and ours up to now is that it was almost destroyed by an F3 tornado in 2002.

Carbon Hill has survived some pretty tough times.

And now they have a mayor who has thrust their town into the national news by posting on social media that the only way to solve society's problems is to kill the LGBT, socialist, and pro-choice among us.

So why mention this? Why give poor, beleaguered Carbon Hill or its illiberal mayor a second thought? Haven't what's left of them been twisted enough?

Lynchings are tragically a phenomenon of our not-too-distant past. And it is entirely possible there are tailored sheets still hanging in closets here in this county and any one you want to name in Alabama or Mississippi or beyond. And they're still hanging there (metaphorically at least) because the currently scared sheetless owners are waiting under their rocks for enough sociopaths to regain power so they can "solve" all our problems the KKK way once again.

Bigotry has never gone away. But the vicious kind has thankfully been somewhat restrained in recent decades by a more civil society. Now cracks are forming in our civility. Little ones and big ones.

We are at a crossroads in this country. And we must boldly declare what we will not stand for, or we will sheepishly fall into a hole (yes, that kind) which we will not deserve to climb out of.

20190604

If the Good Samaritan
had been a nationalist,
he would not have been
a parable.

If Jesus
had been a nationalist …
what would you be?

20190530

Harmony

Near the end of its previous life, the Princess Theatre in South Pittsburg screened the movie Sleeping Beauty. It was the fifth in a series of cartoon feature films in which Walt Disney had incorporated symphonic music. During the 40s and 50s the theatrical wizard had deftly exposed much of America's working class to this form of culture, rarely available to them otherwise.

Sitting in the same place tonight the memory flashed back of that first movie I ever saw in a theatre. And here among faces from a lifetime of memories we were listening to symphonic music ... live ... at a pinnacle moment of the Princess' rebirth. And the irony was so thick you couldn't cut it with a fork. Because it was certainly nothing less than a concerted effort by so many people in this community to create a venue suitable for an ensemble of classical performers from the big city.

There is so much disharmony in the world today, so much venom, distrust, anger, fear. And yet among this very diverse group, our little burg was feasting on the fruit of collaborative effort.

And you know what ... if we can make it here, we can make it anywhere.

Regardless of the strife across the country, our neighbors in cities big and small would have been heartened tonight to see how well harmony works when enough folks get on the same page together.

20190525

Good Listeners

We said goodbye to a superlative storyteller in South Pittsburg this afternoon. And the scores who sat around her table over the years, either at her home or at Stevarinos on most Friday nights, will tell you she was just as good a listener.

After leaving Christ Church, there was another venue waiting for me in Chattanooga. The theme of the ecumenical event this evening was also story telling. The speakers invited us to consider the value of stories as the best tools for forming relationships, thereby deepening and strengthening the framework of community.

The exercise for the hour was to break into groups of two and tell each other a story. A person you didn't know. Sitting near the back, I decided to join someone who had taken a seat at the very back, by herself. I asked if she wanted me to go first or if she would rather start. After a moment she hesitantly began, vaguely at first, then slowing wading into a childhood nightmare that had affected her every moment since.

Listening to this woman, it was like lightening striking. What I had initially thought to share would have been like a lightening bug in comparison (yes, I borrowed that analogy). Then it occurred to me the trust it took for her to share something like that. Trust I that had not earned, but trust fostered by the multi-denominational faith community brought together for that very purpose.

I was coming up empty with something to share, but she continued talking, much to my relief. She explained how with God's help she had come through the ordeal and had been waiting for God to call her to use her survival experience to help someone else. And then I had something to offer. I told her how my priest frequently dismisses services encouraging parishioners to create quiet moments in our lives, to be alert, but to find moments of silence, "because God is a whisperer." How many chances had gone unheeded by me to be a blessing to someone before that reminder became part of my worship?

Thanks be to God, for good story tellers, especially the ones who teach us how to be better listeners.

20190514

Revelations of Admiration

You can tell a lot about someone by what they laugh at. Also by where they put their time, talent and money. But perhaps the most revealing trait, the clearest subcutaneous window to someone's heart and mind, is who they admire. In this observation we can ascertain what is important to the admirer … and what is not. It may be the best clue, if you will, about someone's values.

Some of my heroes have changed over the years. As a Jaycee in the 70s I was a faithful reader of Success magazine and tried to imitate the habits of the VIPs featured in each issue. Later, after reading more comprehensive biographies on many of them, some of them no longer seemed so compelling to emulate.

Our close friends may know us pretty well, but the majority of our acquaintances have a synopsis at best. And so they fill in the blanks with the clues they collect.

Do the clues you are leaving accurately tell your story? Well, probably.

But if you took a good look at those clues yourself, is there a chance you might prefer a different story?

It's never too late to start writing a new chapter.

20190402

FREE SOUP

Calamitous Cuts

As the push for calamitous cuts in social programs continues to gain momentum, the question many churches are asking is, "How will we be able to respond?" Most are doing all they can already to help our neighbors deal with a lack of food, medicine, shelter and other basic necessities.

Churches are asking. But at the same time those who blame our nation's problems on the wretched refuse among us are declaring imperatively that it's not the government's job to help them. They say churches should and will have to take care of them as our government gets out of the welfare business.

Let's see. If you divide the amount of money our government currently spends on social safety net programs by the number of churches in the country, that comes to just under $2 million per congregation. How well would that number fit into your church's annual benevolence budget?

A century ago in this country it was standard operating procedure for people to starve to death. Churches, then as now, did all they could. But starvation was commonplace; destitution ubiquitous. We the people had not yet found our collective strength. We did not fully understand the order of magnitude lying dormant within us, waiting to be summoned by challenges long thought impossible.

Government is not them versus us. Our government is us and capable of far greater things than any one of us can possibly attempt. And so now knowing to a somewhat greater degree what we are capable of, how dare we hang our head and tuck our tail and do less?!

Yes there are abuses which should be corrected, but fractional in comparison to the dole at the other end of the economic spectrum. When everybody liked Ike, that raving socialist under whose watch our citizens and corporations paid taxes based on how well they were doing, we hit our stride in great achievements and continued to do so through the 70s. The Great Society may not have been fully realized, but we came within sight of it before the paradigm began to shift.

A perfect government is not possible. But a perfect storm is. Speaking of coming within sight of something, remember December of 2008? A perfect storm was about to rip our economy to pieces until the dark horse candidate not yet sworn into office stepped up and began to help quell the maelstrom. That disaster, thankfully averted, was the result of greed, not unlike our current disposition. Will we be so fortunate on our next visit to the precipice?

20190328

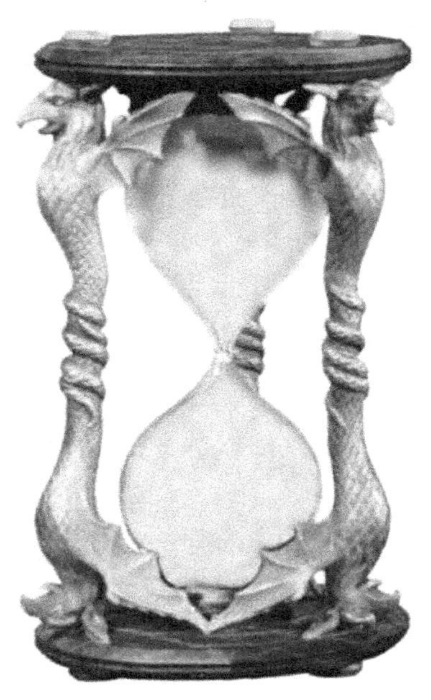

An opaque hourglass
with an unknown quantity of sand.

The question is not
how much time is left?
The question is
what are you doing with the time?

20190323

Self-made?

"He was a self-made man. After attending public schools, he worked his way up ..." Wait! We've all read bios like this countless times. It is high time we stopped the false narrative in its tracks. "Self-made" is true on the rarest of occasions, perhaps as often as being raised by wolves. Even those who never set foot in a public school certainly use public streets, rely on the fire department, and avail themselves of community in countless ways.

Our Declaration of Independence was from tyranny, not from each other. Our greatness comes from our interdependence. Solos have their place, but we make our best music in concert.

I had an incredible conversation the other day with someone who had overcome cancer and then needed hip replacement due to bone loss from the chemo. Though receiving disability at the moment, he is back to work part time and determined to return to full time employment. Inspiring. But the incredible part of the conversation was his belief that socialism is ruining our country and must be eliminated if we're ever to be great again.

The safety nets that catch us when we are knocked down, as well as the systems we put in place to build each other up, should not be viewed as signs of weakness. They are integral parts of what makes us so strong. They comprise the framework that has made the middle class possible for the past century.

I look in the mirror every morning and only observe the half I once was. Conversely the camera is not my friend. Go figure. Maybe it works like the strong delusion Paul mentioned to the Thessalonians. Nope. Neither God nor Paul effected my waistline, nor did they put scales on my eyes (pun intended). I have no one to blame but myself when I refuse to see the truth right in front of me. Our current national delusion, on the other hand, is sent by a higher power, and we believe their subterfuge at great peril.

For aristocracy to be completely restored to the former glory of the Gilded Age or the ruling classes of previous centuries, they must first fully repopulate serfdom. Student loan debt is one contemporary version of indentured servitude. Medical bankruptcy is another. Both will pale in comparison, though, when the gutting of public schools achieves cruising speed and the dismantling of Social Security crosses the failsafe point.

Storm cloud's a comin'. And behind that cloud is not a silver lining.

It is oligarchy (a.k.a. tyranny).

20190319

EMERGENCY
BROADCAST
SYSTEM

An Eternal Inward Struggle

The duck and cover drills were fading by the time I started South Pittsburg Elementary School. But the Emergency Broadcast System was still in full swing on television. There was no escaping the reminder that we lived in the Atomic Age and at any given moment we could all be vaporized.

But like the static snow on TV after midnight, the EBS tests eventually became just noise, nothing to really worry about. You might say the stress finally calloused over and we went on with our lives. Or course it helped that the deadly flash never happened here.

There's an irony about hearing something over and over. Some of the scariest figures the world has ever known used this human coping mechanism to their own iniquitous advantage. Truth isn't required; facts non-essential. Simply repeat something often enough about individuals or groups your audience has little contact with, offer assurance that things would be better except for "them," and acceptance predictably sets in.

We have slaughtered savages to make room for family farms, enslaved dark-skinned fractional humans to expedite our agricultural pursuits, exploited countless other ethnic groups as we forged through the industrial age, sent a preponderance of our poor to die in battles around the world, and yet again are paying onerous tribute to the invisible elite who have from the beginning told us over and over what (and who) we need to dispense with if we ever hope to be great.

You may think I'm talking about one person. I'm not. I'm talking about us. We the people, unconsciously waiting for the next signal to get rid of the next alleged threat to our security, comfort and convenience. Evil is not just lurking out there in the dark. Evil also lurks within each of us. To overcome evil is not a singular outward battle; it is an eternal inward struggle.

What does lurk out there in the dark is the next set of greedy bastards exciting us to do their dirty work for them. They don't send engraved invitations. Their subtle signals may be a set of crosshairs on someone's picture, or a magazine photo with the headline "Target Practice."

The better angels of our nature are working overtime as we edge perilously close to the fail-safe point beyond the rule of law. However strongly you may disagree, surely you would never use these tactics. The whole point of this missive is … if you would make excuses for those who do use these tactics, your better angels may be on their last legs.

20190225

Sophistry

I used to believe in Santa Claus. At a certain point early in elementary school, the fantasy was crushed and thus began the drudgerous hike up the hill of realism.

Parents revel in the delight of children and this warm, fuzzy custom. They would find it troublesome, though, if their offspring continued believing the artifice into adulthood. The joke often is that older children will gladly pretend to believe as long as the gifts keep coming. But to actually never come to grips with reality would become a serious problem.

Sophistry is not a concept six-year olds need to wrestle with. But they certainly need to learn to recognize it as they acclimate into maturity. If you couldn't identify it, you would fall for anything, blindly believe whatever someone said, foolishly follow whatever seemed most appealing.

At the moment, the separation of powers may be melting faster than glacial ice. This is not a Republican versus Democrat thing. This is a republic versus dystopic thing. Those who think they're getting what they want aren't noticing the Christmas tree and the roast beast disappearing up the chimney. The Capitol building is not on fire, but we have a declared emergency just the same where both sides of the aisle could find themselves sidelined if they don't react quickly.

Some of the sharpest conservative minds in the country are saying the same thing right now. They are concerned. We all should be.

20190215

On the Record

We all make mistakes. We all say things we later wish we hadn't. Things said in public meetings are more likely remembered than things said in bars. Points made repeatedly are more likely recalled than things said incidentally.

Then there's the written word. Ideas and opinions put in writing need not rely on memory for a clear recollection, just the document. One off letters between two people add some responsibility and consequence, but to really take ownership of an idea, media is where true risk and reward lives.

Gutenberg shifted the paradigm. Of course there were those who could afford scribes before the tech revolution of movable type, but forever after communication has continued to get faster and broader as the world has gotten better and worse, richer and poorer.

For nearly 400 years mass communication was reserved for the elite. In the last century or so journalism found much broader outlets. But only in the last generation has information moved from consumer product to a fully participatory medium.

Here is a thought. When you participate … in writing … even if no paper and ink is involved … even if you later hit the delete key for hours on end … it's too late to deny … it's too late to hide. You have joined the ranks of "on the record" with inescapable commensurate responsibility.

And here is the point. We should make the best possible use of social (and other forms of fully accessible mass) media. But we should do so carefully with discernment. Copying or sharing someone else's opinion or agenda without being certain if it is factual, without being sure of the source, can be very dangerous and damaging. And if/when things do get broken and/or people do get hurt, will you feel as strongly then about the opinion you didn't take time to contemplate and express for yourself?

Reckless does come home to roost.

20190214

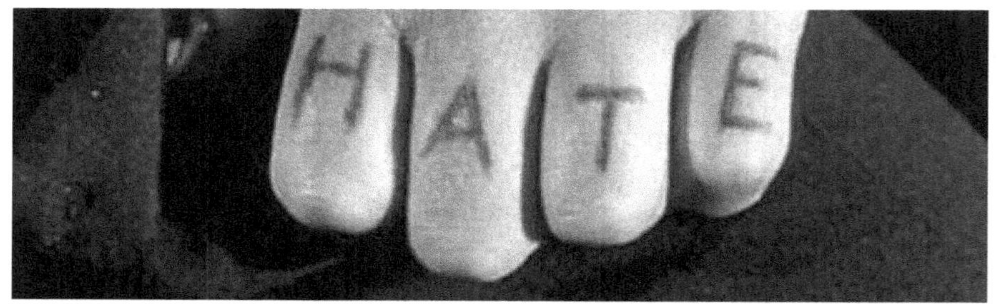
HATE

Hate Groups

Friends of mine have been sharing a big red post on Facebook this week about the largest hate group in America ... one that I belong to. It is the hate group responsible for the Social Security checks many of those friends cash each month. It is the same hate group responsible for the program which helps pay many of their medical bills.

Oddly enough, I don't hate the fact that they are benefitting from these programs, nor do I hate them, even though I often disagree with them.

20190207

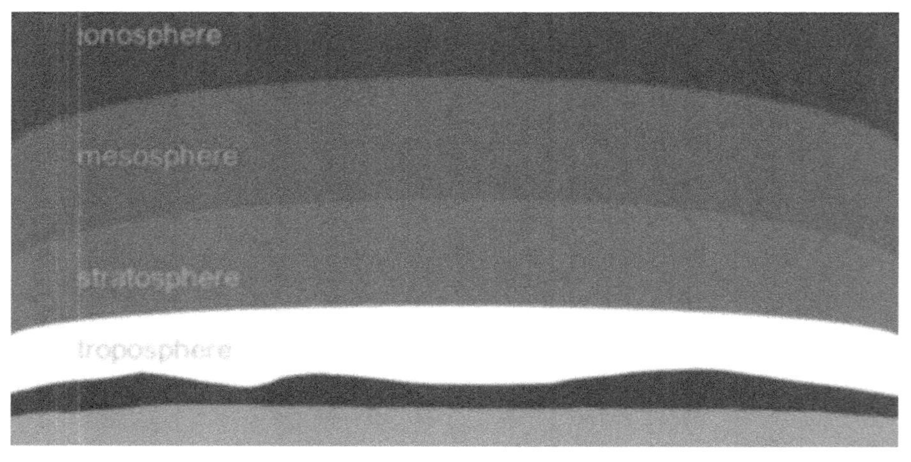
ionosphere
mesosphere
stratosphere
troposphere

Down Here at Ground Level

Not everyone is fortunate enough to live in the South Pittsburg SMSA. There are a host of benefits, not the least of which is our very own, reasonably priced, variety-packed coffee bar. Dragging Canoe doesn't have a shop on every corner, but they are just around the corner from every place downtown.

The downside is I can't regularly boycott that grossly overpriced mega-chain whose former CEO and brand-maker, Howard Schultz, is now planning to run as an independent in the 2020 presidential election. All I can do, I guess, is when I am out of town and drive past one of those places, to just keep driving (as is usually my custom anyway).

Schultz may actually have a good idea or two. He is genuinely accomplished. And he can put words together, even sentences and thoughts, that actually make sense. He probably wouldn't be an embarrassment. Nor would he ever have the chance, running as an independent. All he can hope to accomplish is (and you can conclude for yourself if this is his intention) to throw the election to the incumbent. With notable exceptions, billionaires live to out-yacht one another while the rest of the country tries to survive on 1970s wages (adjusted for inflation ... maybe). Maintaining the status quid pro quo would not be detrimental to Mr. Schultz, who along with his peers has already saved enough in tax relief in the last year or so to keep Congress on retainer for the foreseeable future.

You might sardonically ask if anti-wealth is now acceptable bigotry? Premise rejected. Billionaires are people, too, and worthy of the same respect as anyone else. It is the very small group who abuse power and privilege at the expense of the working class who must be reined in and required to send their money to Washington the same way the rest of us do, through taxes, not gratuities.

Those of my friends who disagree; you have rich friends. So do I. But none of us have friends who own tropical islands and manipulate markets. There is such a thing as too much money in the hands of too few. And absolute power does corrupt absolutely. Sadly these truths are not evident to all of us in the troposphere. Hopefully enough of us learn before it is too late that self-government is a rare gift which can be taken away ... even forfeited.

20190201

Better Questions

At one time or another, in one way or another, each of us has made a difference. Often for the better. That is prudent investment.

At other times and places, each of us has just made noise. Perhaps with a desire, but no true expectation or likelihood of making a difference. That is hollow expense.

There is a popular theory that to become truly proficient at something, one must spend at least ten thousand hours in study and practice. Certainly one has to be dedicated to spending that kind of time at anything. But an unsettling question comes to mind: what if you spent ten thousand hours practicing something the wrong way? Would you get any points for all the effort? Or would you just be preeminently inadequate?

How do we find the best answers? For far too many of us too much of the time, the approach is to become louder and angrier in our pursuit. What we seem to have forgotten in our vitriol is simply to ask better questions.

As we pummel each other senseless, a small, obscenely wealthy group of people outside the public eye pushes our buttons about immigrants, guns, abortion and other highly emotional topics. Through social media and other subversive marketing means, they continually provoke us to ask the wrong questions, to practice the wrong things. And we keep fighting, much to their delight, and keep losing, much to their exponential benefit.

The question is about better immigration policy.

The question is about better firearm regulation.

The question is about better abortion alternatives.

We could be making tremendous strides in each of these areas, but instead we allow ourselves to be pushed to the extreme fringes of each issue where failure holds us hostage.

If we wish to quit making noise and start making progress, we might stop listening to the noise and start focusing again on attainable goals.

20190129

SOLO
BLANCOS

The New Jim Crow

Why aren't we afraid of Canadians? Why does a 5500-mile border not worry us nearly so much as a 1900 mile one? If it's Middle Eastern terrorists we're worried about, wouldn't it actually be smarter for them to fly into Edmonton and stroll across than to fly into Tijuana where border security is much tighter?

There are some who see the battle for the wall as this century's version of Jim Crow. Some say Canadian immigration causes no concern because it doesn't make us darker. Those observations may make you mad. But if they do, why do they? Are you offended by bigotry? Or are you disturbed to wonder if maybe there are vestiges of prejudice still lingering just behind the pale face in the mirror.

We should be concerned with hostile foreigners trying to infiltrate this country and we do all we can (at least we did until recently) to screen our airports, patrol our coastlines. monitor our cyber security, etc.

A much greater threat to our collective safety today is crumbling infrastructure. We need to be rebuilding and improving roads and bridges that make our economy possible, yet it often takes us longer today to get to Chattanooga than before I-24 was built. Are we making progress, or have we forgotten what that word means?

What is dominating our attention in the Rio Grande region at the moment is not a wall, not a crisis, not an issue. It is smoke and mirrors diverting attention away from the window of opportunity for the very rich to get very much richer while the rest of the country, conservatives and liberals alike, lose more and more ground every day that our children (perhaps even our grandchildren) may not have the chance to recover.

Have you ever watched a cat chase the red dot from a laser pointer across the floor? Not so funny anymore as we realize we have become that cat.

20190119

Encouragers

Not a single person I ever knew was able to leap tall buildings in a single bound. I've met a handful of people who have appeared on the network news, but the vast majority of the folks I've known lived outside the national spotlight. And yet, greatness lives among us, often unassuming.

Standing in queue yesterday to speak to Helen and the rest of the Brooks' family, you could hear a multitude of stories about Sam; inspiring, funny, touching, familiar stories. But the line didn't stretch out into the parking lot because of any one of those stories. The honor was for the cumulative effect of his habitual caring about other people and looking for ways to encourage them. Those he coached weren't just ballplayers. Those he taught weren't just students. Those he met in any other venue … not just … more than. And he took the time to help people see and become the "more than" within themselves

So how do we honor such greatness? How do we cope with the loss of someone who touched so many lives in so many ways?

To honor Sam Brooks, to prevent his passing from leaving our corner of the world less than it was, we can follow his great example of looking for the best in others and not just see it but encourage it. And each time you lift someone up, you soar just a little higher, just like Sam did.

201812229

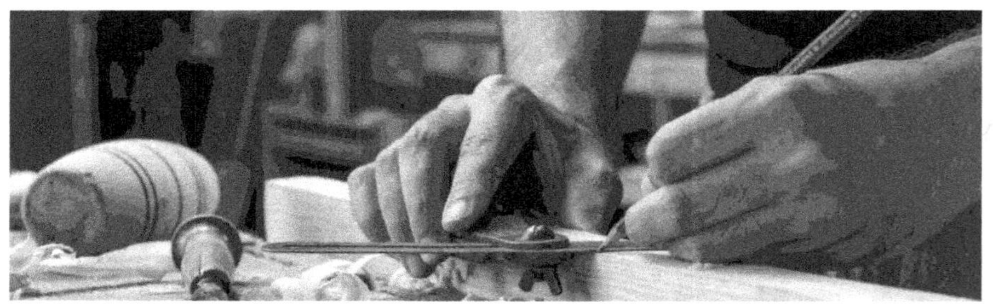

Epiphanies

When something was broken, there was a time I would try to fix it. More often than not it ultimately cost more for someone else to finally come make the repair than it would have if I had called them straight away. Realization eventually occurred that I was not handy. Thereafter life became less frustrating because I focused my attentions on things, I was better suited to do.

As my children were growing up the temptation was great to discourage them from things, I wasn't good at. After all, the acorn doesn't fall far from the tree, so why let them waste their time, like I had so often, on things they couldn't be good at.

An epiphany helped me reconsider. One of the heretical writers I followed at that time offered a different perspective on Proverbs 22:6 - "Train up a child in the way he should go..." He suggested rather than pushing a child to become your vision, to follow your path, to think as you think and do as you do, you might allow their interests and talents the chance to form, then encourage and support them in those directions ... not yours.

Today I have a grown son who can build or fix just about anything, maybe because I learned it might not be the best idea to tell him he wouldn't be good at that. Now he is the one I call. And he's usually ready to rise to just about any challenge.

The other son ... he likes to put words together. A craftsman in his own right. And he's not shy about challenges, either.

In all my years of challenges and opportunities, I have learned that one of the greatest blessings you can ever enjoy is reverse mentoring.

20181222

A STEP AHEAD
FOUNDATION

A Step Ahead Foundation

A most-wanted pregnancy. Celebrated for some 20 centuries by millions of Christians around the world. And before this common era, anticipated and longed for by millions more at least as many centuries aforetime. Those of us who observe Advent take time to reflect each year on that one who was born ... and for what purpose ... and for what purpose we are called now.

In discerning our purpose, some feel imitation is the sincerest form of spirituality, and so ministers to ones less fortunate than ourselves ranks highly on our to be list. But aid need not always be reactive. We can also respond in proactive ways ... helping to avoid adversity before it strikes.

What if there was a proven process to reduce poverty and improve educational and economic opportunities for families in our communities rather than reacting to perpetual privation? Would that not prove to be better for all concerned?

There is an organization which not only has such a vision but has demonstrated momentous results by providing better access to reversible birth control, thereby decreasing unwanted pregnancies and the consequential hardships which beget poverty. This accordingly increases positive pregnancy outcomes for healthier families when the time is right.

That organization, A Step Ahead Foundation, was conceived by a juvenile judge in Memphis, Tennessee. Claudia Swafford Haltom had seen enough despair during her 17 years on the bench where unplanned pregnancies had eliminated opportunities for young women to avoid or escape poverty. Rather than put that pain and suffering out of her mind upon retirement in 2011, she imagined ways and coordinated means to provide highly effective birth control to women in her community who could not afford it. And the success of the program quickly grew beyond Shelby County, now helping women all across Tennessee.

Of course there are some who object to contraception, and that belief should be respected for all who choose not to use it. At the same time, those who see the benefits of an assisted shift towards a higher percentage of wanted pregnancies in our communities might consider what they can do to help make this clemency possible. And it is possible. We simply must purpose to be proactive.

Could there be a better time?

201891218

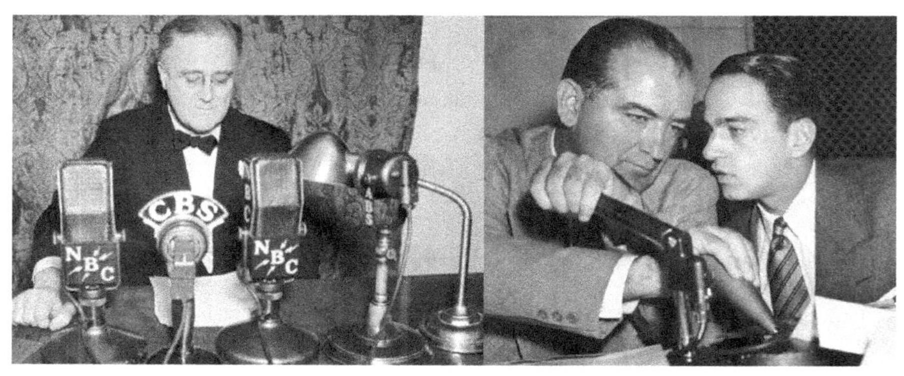
NBC
CBS
NBC

A First-Century Conspiracy?

Several prestigious university studies may have uncovered a vast first-century conspiracy.

You may have heard there are 365 verses in the Bible which encourage (or command) us to "fear not." Some scholars say that's not entirely accurate because sometimes the wording is "do not fear," or some other variation. And other passages about not fearing might fall into a slightly different contextual mold. At any rate, we can surely agree "fear not" is a continuing theme in both the Old and New Testaments.

Research at the University of Nebraska, New York University, and Yale University, among others, has recently identified the correlation of fear and a conservative mindset. Brain scans have found that the amygdala, which is the fear center of the brain, is usually larger in conservatives than in liberals. A series of other laboratory studies have also shown that when adult liberals experienced a physical threat, their attitudes (both political and social) became more conservative (at least temporarily).

Then there is our own unscientific observation of fearmongering. Who has not witnessed and grimaced at such unsavory oratory or activity at one time or another?

There is a difference, of course, between a cautionary tale and baseless inflammatory rhetoric. To warn someone to be careful is not the same thing as using scare tactics to create phobias of certain groups of people. The images in our heads might give us a clue about our phrenic tendencies. Which portrait hangs in your cerebral chapel: gun-toting Jesus or peace-loving Jesus? As you know, there are no original illustrations in the Bible, so we imagine as we will from what we read and how we interpret it. The closest we come to finding Jesus brandishing a sword is when he restores Malchus' ear after Peter's impulsive swordplay.

What we think is often influenced by who we listen to (or what we read), whether we question and contemplate it ... or not.

So is the mantra of "Fear Not" a centuries-old left-wing plot to make us all more liberal? I wouldn't be too anxious about it (scriptural pun intended). But praying for courage in trying times is never a bad idea.

20181205

Thankful

I am thankful for friends I disagree with:

The present tense ones who remain friends despite our differences.

The past tense ones who taught me I could survive without trying to please everyone.

The future tense ones yet to cross my path who will bring new strengths to the framework that friendship is.

The pluperfect ones who are gone, but not forgotten, whose alternatives made me think harder and gain confidence in my ideas ... and sometimes helped me change my mind.

The encouraging ones who welcome healthy conversation.

The quiet ones who focus on things in common.

The clamorous ones who invigorate volition.

And even the friends who don't realize they are yet are woven into the blessings of a life I give thanks for today and always.

20181122

Compassionate Society

A compassionate message is making its way around social media this Thanksgiving week:

"Can't feed 'em, don't breed 'em.

The government is not your baby's daddy."

Yes, there are those who work the system and abuse the safety nets in place. But for every food stamp spent on a candy bar (no, you can't buy beer and cigarettes with SNAP), there are multiple dollars spent on corporate welfare. And many people on food stamps are working multiple jobs to try to take care of their families. Others face the dilemma of losing Medicaid if they earn "too much" at a job that doesn't offer access to health insurance or pay enough to cover the rent and groceries.

When a society reaches the point where it likens some of its citizens to animals, it is well on its way to forfeiting its claim to be a society.

20181119

Bells

I remember first hearing the different sound from the church tower during the funeral service for a close friend several years ago. It was the same bell I'd heard many times before, but the sound was somber, like the mood below. Odd how a sound can catch in your throat. It appropriately punctuated the good-bye to a mentor who had challenged me to do more and be more than I had intended in a particularly risky volunteer pursuit. Forever after, that muffled peal at a funeral reminds me, not of loss, but appreciation for those who have gone the extra mile.

Another time was a memorial service at a different church for a couple I did not know but knew of. Their car had been swept away in a flood. They were headed to church to take care of details often taken for granted when someone quietly goes about doing extra-mile things. The memorial was in a garden beside the church, which had bells that automatically played at set times on Sunday. As fate would have it, they began to play right in the middle of the memorial service. The priest at first tried to talk over the chimes, but finally stopped and asked if anyone knew how to stop the ringing. The parishioners looked at one another, then someone pointed to the urn.

Each of us have opportunities every day to go the extra mile for someone or some cause we give ourselves to. When we do, we are being the world we want to live in. We are the wether, wearing the bell, that others may follow to a place hopefully made better by our concerted effort.

20181116

Safety First

I learned to drive in my grandmother's '66 Malibu Super Sport. How in the world my 70-year-old grandmother bought that car has always been a mystery to me? Not that I had much of a chance to get in trouble with it. If it had ever been spotted doing more than 30 mph around town, Miss Alma would have answered a hundred phone calls at The Hustler office in five minutes. Plus, I wasn't supposed to take it out of town (notice how carefully-constructed that sentence is). And Grandmother's primary rule was that it should never have more than 1/4 of a tank of gas ... so if it was stolen the thief couldn't get all the way to Florida before having to stop.

The economy usually runs on a full tank of gas ... until recession hits. Then we run on fumes for months or years. What we're seeing at the moment is the trailing end of a very long bull market cycle. The last recovery started slow but had a healthy, sustained run. Now as interest rates begin to rise, the trend may taper or it may topple, but correction is coming.

This is not about who gets the credit or who gets blamed. This is about making good decisions now. Do you cut the safety net when the trapeze flyer is getting tired, or is that when the net is needed most?

Sacking social security at the worst possible moment as markets inevitably correct will ensure that millions and millions of people will be ruined. This is not a chance. This is a choice.

20181104

Interdependence

Each of us had help. Every footstep forward, every handhold upward, made possible by something other than ourselves. Foundations and frameworks, built by our predecessors, enabled us to climb.

Independence is a myth. Interdependence is the reality. Look at your resume. Most of it is not about you, it is about all the opportunities you had to become who you are. And what you acknowledged is only the tip of the iceberg.

There is a name for this framework: community.

As we better ourselves, are we making the path easier or harder for those who follow? Some purpose to strengthen the rungs as they climb, others try to pull the ladders up behind them, hoarding the benefits for themselves. That is not community, that is gluttony.

20181103

Obfuscation

Hating someone accomplishes nothing of value. What good is it to hate someone because of their hateful rhetoric? You both end up in the ditch.

And if that doesn't give you pause for thought, please consider that when we are vocal in our hatred of someone, regardless of how justified we may be, we give them cover to confuse whatever point we're trying to make. Who wins when attention is focused on your frenzied reaction rather than the real issue?

You probably know what obfuscation is. Even if you do, please go to Dictionary.com right now and look it up. It's a helluva word, even more so when you see that its root means "to darken." And while you're there, check out the synonyms.

Much has been done of late to dismantle what has taken lifetimes to build for the greater good of our society. And those who have profited have done so with very little scrutiny. How? Because we're busy swatting at shadows and shiny objects rather than focusing on what's really happening. That's not somebody else's fault. That's our fault.

We need to take ownership of what has happened and chart a new course for what needs to happen. There will be more shiny objects … count on it, but don't fall for it anymore. It is time to send the demolition crews home and hire new builders who will help us get back to the business of building neighborhoods that children of every color, creed, race and religion can live in together peacefully and happily.

And that has never been the result of hating.

20181028

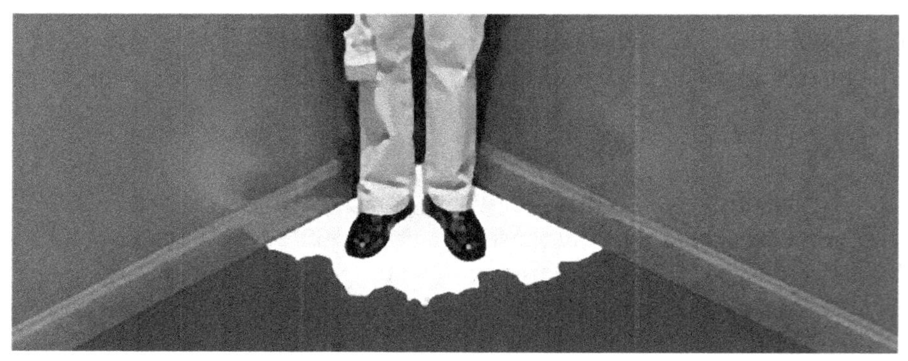

Labels

White, not supremacist.
Male, not misogynist.
Christian, not sinless.
American, not nationalist.
Democrat, not indentured.
Liberal, not infallible.
Patriotic, not myopic.
Privileged, not entitled.

Sometimes we seem to be painted into a corner by the labels we wear, or the labels others apply to us. And sometimes we categorize others by who we think they are. Life is not black and white, nor is it one particular polarized color.

Each of us wear coats of many colors and have complex views on a variety of subjects. And it is okay to change our minds sometimes, hopefully after thinking more deeply about an issue … or a person.

According to scripture, God changed his mind on occasion. If he can, maybe we can, too.

20181027

Prayer in the First Person

After reading about the pipe bomb incidents today, I reached for my BCP. That's not an assault weapon, it's the Book of Common Prayer.

"O God, the Father of all, whose Son commanded us to love our enemies: Lead them and us from prejudice to truth: deliver them and us from hatred, cruelty, and revenge; and in your good time enable us all to stand reconciled before you, through Jesus Christ our Lord. Amen."

This is not an easy prayer on a good day. It's even tougher today or any day when we are upset by evil action in the world. But such is the time when expansive prayer is most needed and perhaps most effectual.

It is so easy to gather up swords or start throwing rocks when we are angry or afraid. Not so easy to pray for understanding on how we might reduce the vitriol in the world by starting in the first person singular.

20181024

VALUE
ME

Signs

Secretly taping a "Kick Me" sign on someone's back. You may have done it as a kid; you probably witnessed it; you might have experienced it. A childish prank. The risk was minimal; not very likely the victim would actually be kicked to death. If you were a bully, it could also get you points for being someone to watch out for.

What does that behavior grow into? Spend five minutes on social media and you find out. Polite society isn't so polite behind a screen. And school-yard bullies … the ones who could write (not necessarily spell) … abound.

But then there are the nice people who become not so nice. They don't use the "N" word, but some feel pretty comfortable throwing the "L" word around. For the record, liberals aren't insulted by being called a liberal, which is probably why the label is then sometimes combined with caustic terms such as "Godless."

I know I don't become Godless by being called Godless. What bothers me, though, are the people I've seen called that often enough who finally became convinced it must be so. Democrats (and other prodigals) I used to worship with who don't go to church anymore. When you're made to feel unwelcome long enough, you eventually shake the mendacity off your feet and leave. The irony is, most of us prodigals know we aren't without sin.

Here's a good exercise. Write down your objective for any task you approach (even if you just do it in your head). Is your goal to learn something when you watch the news, or is it just to find the things you agree with? Is your intention when you share something on Facebook to make a friend smile, or to make them think, or is it to call someone a depreciative name? Do you look for opportunities to invite disparate people to your church or your civic group or your home or is it your aim to make sure they understand that they would be happier somewhere else? This is not me trying to be being smart. This is me trying to share lessons others have taught me. This is the result of 35 years of sanding and polishing by my wife and my sons … and my daughter-in-law … and my grandkids, who have all gone to great lengths to turn a lump of clay into a pot that now tries his best every day to say something effectual to the kettles I meet.

We all have value. Who is best qualified to measure it?

God more … we less.

20181022

Losing Ground

If your neighbor builds a fence inside your property line and you don't dispute it, a few years from now they can file a claim to own that strip of land. It's called "adverse possession."

Right now millions of Americans are forfeiting their right to vote, but millions more who are still voting are also at risk. Yes, you. First, if you don't register, you don't get to vote. They don't automatically register you to vote when you sign up for Amazon Prime. Second, even if you register, if you blow off going to vote multiple times (varies by state) they will purge you from the rolls.

Then there are those who try to register and vote but are denied for various reasons. If you read/watch the news, you are aware of voter suppression. This is not a new phenomenon. The haves aren't evil people (usually), but in every generation we have seen them use laws and rules and shenanigans to keep the have-nots from voting. Are you a have or a have-not? If you think you are a have and thereby insulated from this practice, remember you have not billions of dollars to buy control of the government and so you should be doing all you can to help your fellow have-nots preserve democracy.

Then there is gerrymandering. Your vote is devalued when elected officials get to pick their voters. A guaranteed losing vote is not really a vote. Then there's the Electoral College, which can and has abrogated the majority vote twice in the last twenty years. Then there's the Citizens United decision, which lets global corporations pretend to be people in the campaign arena ... not unlike the Philadelphia Eagles vs the local Junior Varsity team. Corporations can't vote ... yet ... but they can drown out everybody else in the room so that only their puppets' voices are heard. Then there's foreign interference in our elections ... depending on who you believe ... from countries that only pretend to let their people vote.

You may think our voting rights are guaranteed. That's not exactly accurate. Our voting rights are assured by our present form of government, so long as our government is impelled by the people to ensure fairness. At the moment there are cracks in that foundation such as previously noted. It will only get worse unless all of us get better at using our votes to resist plutocracy ... or oligarchy ... or worse.

Adverse possession of our voting rights is possible. Sit quietly and do nothing and see.

No, please don't. GO VOTE!

20181018

Don't Just Stand There

Someone comes up to you in a dimly lit parking lot, puts a gun in your face and takes your money. Or somebody breaks into your house and steals your valuables. You can call the police. If the thief is caught, they will be arrested. If not, at least there is hopefully insurance to indemnify you.

But what if someone has a license to steal? What if they have the authority to reach into your account and take a chunk of your hard-earned retirement savings? The groundwork is being laid as we speak. There will be no policeman to call and nowhere to file a claim. And there is no fence you can build that will protect you.

There is one recourse available, though, to prevent this crime before it happens. You can vote tomorrow through November 6 to replace those in Washington who are planning the biggest heist in our history. Social Security and Medicare are not entitlements and those funds should not be embezzled to cover the billions of dollars recently gifted to the biggest of campaign contributors.

Maybe you're young and you don't expect to ever benefit from Social Security. You might be right. But not voting now only increases the likelihood things will get that bad or worse later on. And what about your aunt in the nursing home … or what about your mom who may still try to retire in a couple of years on the vestige of a pension lacerated in the next Wall Street crash? This touches us all, today and tomorrow. The good news is … we have the power to stop it.

Now before you try to make the case that Congress does the same thing when they tax us, don't. Taxes are part of a contract with our country to make civilized society possible. Each of us renews the agreement every time we step on a sidewalk. FICA is a separate mutually agreed contract … and we have kept our part of the bargain. The Social Security trust fund is not the problem. Corruption is at the root of our spiraling deficit.

We have work to do. Don't just stand there with your hands up waiting to be robbed. Capitol Hill still belongs to all of us, not just a privileged few. Go vote!

20181016

Evil Mr. Rogers

So I had not seen the Fox & Friends clip discussing "this evil, evil man Mr. Rogers" until today when I was reading about the new Tom Hanks movie. The clip isn't recent, but it does help me understand a little better why half this country hates the other half. CNN is not faultless. I rarely listen to their panel discussions anymore, but I try not to miss their very professionally done specials such as the annual CNN Heroes program. Roger Ailes, on the other hand, produced nothing of merit, in my plebeian opinion, from the day Rupert Murdock hired him til his career faded to black a couple of years ago.

If Fred Rogers is evil, then I want to be evil, too. I grew up smoking cigarettes and watching Captain Kangaroo, but my kids grew up with Mr. Rogers on PBS. They loved him then and I love him still. He filled in the gaps of the good example I wanted to be. A minister at heart, he showed us, children and adults, how to bring Sunday School out into the street.

People sometimes said unkind things to (or about) my dad, because the editor of the local paper wasn't always going to make everybody happy. He taught me to deal with insults in the first person, but I never quite got there when they criticized him. Watching the Fox Friends vilify Mr. Rogers reminded me of that old feeling. I will go to my grave remembering hateful words I saw my dad set aside with a calmness forever out of my reach.

Fortunately, Mr. Rogers left us before having to hear the Fox Friends call him evil. But if he had, I'm sure he would have turned to us, smiled and said, "Imagine what our real neighborhoods would be like if each of us offered, as a matter of course, just one kind word to another person."

20181011

Golden Calves

A young son of an agnostic puts on a wool suit, mounts a maiden pulpit, and in just a few years grows a small flock into a prosperous mega-church. And that just for starters. He also converts his flock and a host of others into the most formidable American voting bloc of the century.

Agree with it, disagree with it, love it or hate it ... however you consider it, you can't ignore it. Fundamentalist Christianity was fundamentally changed. And the Republican Party was patently transposed. In my humble estimation, the vast majority of those swept up in the movement put their backs into the effort with a sincere desire to make manifest the teachings of their Lord and Savior Jesus Christ. And the result was almost unbelievable.

If you want to see a movie about epic evangelism, watch The Founder. It is the story of the McDonalds phenomenon. But as you probably know, the phenom was really a Kroc. The great little idea underwent drastic changes after Ray Kroc discovered the original, simple diner. What you see today is like it, but not. The miracle worker made millions, the organization made billions, but the soul of the McDonald brothers was forever lost in that transubstantiation.

Some say the conservative movement can never escape the gravitational pull of the black hole they have fallen into orbit around. I say that ... almost as frequently as the next news cycle. But I could be wrong. And I hope I am. Not that I see myself returning to either of those groups, but because I have dear friends in (if you can still say both).

I think there are compassionate conservatives capable, though perhaps still not willing at the moment, to fight for and take their party back. I think there are provincial Christians who are finally beginning to notice the conspicuous absence of Christian virtues in the political debacles that bloody them almost daily.

Our current predicament may get better. But it could become very much worse. The devils may tremble at your faith, but Authoritarianism isn't flinching. There is too much money and power to ignore. And should it ultimately break through and steal, there won't be enough Democracy left for a moth to make a meal of.

Will we continue to bow to golden calves or will we stand up and vote for what we used to call principles? Our next chance could be our last chance.

20181010

What's Behind the Anger?

We sometimes fret about those who can't speak up for themselves. Then we typically commence to putting words in their mouths. Occasionally that's the noble thing to do. More often we would do better to be quiet with them.

In a sermon I heard recently was a suggestion that we append to every opinion we offer, "but I could be wrong." At that moment my inner child stomped his foot on my cerebellum and shouted, "but I'm not!" I imagined there was a silent chorus of similar inner voices in the room, but ...

I read a litany of comments on one especially vicious online conversation today, many wishing Justice Ruth Bader Ginsburg would drop dead soon.

The take-away for me was being relieved not to be what they claimed to be. But that's not entirely accurate. I strive not to be. But I have been. Left to my own devices, I could be again.

Who is not a product of their environment? Your accent and your expressions are only two of a host of proofs that you have been influenced by others. Parentage may be a given, though not always in the fortunate sense ... extremely fortunate in my case, and that just for starters. A brother and a sister who have both helped me make course corrections over the years. A wife who unknowingly helped keep me from burning the bridge with God and then ten thousand angel moments since. Two sons and a daughter-in-law who never cease to amaze or encourage me. I am a fortunate one, yes. So many others in this polarized, angry society are not so fortunate. To grow up in deprivation, if not resources then perhaps affection or attention or even darker circumstance. In such places anger can put down roots and the fruit can be bitter or even poisonous. When we fail to consider that, we truly have a failure to communicate.

Is it our intention to have two groups who evidently hate each other at the expense of the nation we share? Surely not. Of course we can't mend every fence or right every wrong or correct every mistake, but can we not find a way to attempt to do so just a little less destructively?

The next time you absolutely disagree with someone about something and you feel your face begin to flush, ask yourself what's behind the angry face across from you. Is it incarnate evil, or is it pain?

When someone wishes someone else would die, the quick response is to call them a moron. Maybe the better idea would be to set aside the angry emoji and just say nothing at all. I am trying, but I need to do better.

By the way, at the risk of being heard to say we should never speak up ... may God bless Ruth Bader Ginsburg ... and be gracious to those who hate her.

20181005

It's Not Their Money!

There are some in Congress who claim "entitlements" such as Social Security are what's driving up the national deficit. That's a lie. Social Security is a federally managed retirement fund that has been paid into by people on the job. When you receive a Social Security check, you are not being taken care of by the government, you are drawing on the retirement account you and your employer paid into for years. The reason Social Security can be confused with tax revenue is because Congress "borrowed" all that money and filled the trust fund with IOUs. So in their convoluted thinking, that converted it into tax dollars to do with as they please.

There are other social programs which assist people in poverty and there are abuses in those programs that need to be addressed. But the dollars per abuser are minuscule in comparison to the entitlements doled out at the other end of the spectrum; corporate welfare far outweighs public assistance to the least of these in our society.

It's not hard to imagine how career autocrats who have their own very generous retirement plan and their own special health care plan can make such callous decisions to cut Social Security, Medicare and other programs that don't affect them one bit. Sitting by a marble fireplace after a heavy meal usually leads to napping, not concern for the cold, wet, hungry people outside.

There are good people in Congress who truly care about the public they serve rather than the billionaires ready to slip them big sweaty wads of money in exchange for legalized tax evasion. They're getting harder to find, but they are there. What they need are more citizens who care to come take the places of the corrupted politicians who don't. That's our job … to send the replacements.

The time-out whistle blows on Tuesday, November 6. There are caring, capable candidates ready to get in the game. Let's send them in!

20181004

We the People

True Courage

I routinely stand and recite the Pledge of Allegiance to the Flag of the United States of America (I noted that last part to avoid any confusion). There are a number of things I take issue within this country and I have found ways of protesting injustices through avenues other than sitting or taking a knee.

I also acknowledge that those whose lips curl when they say the name Kaepernick have a Constitutional right to snarl, or burn their Nikes, or shout obscenities at their TV during NFL pregame ceremonies. After all, it is a freedom afforded them under the Constitution.

Freedom of speech loses its saltiness, though, when it has to pass a litmus test. Not only is freedom for a select few or even the majority an endangered freedom, it is at the same time marching us down a dangerous path. When any particular group is allowed to muzzle or suppress another group, freedom of speech has become counterfeit or, to finish the initial analogy, has been trampled underfoot.

Consider the case of the Texas teen who is facing the wrath of the state's Attorney General this week for refusing to stand for the Pledge at her school. What is she protesting? Not sure. Doesn't matter. What does matter is the civics lesson she is learning: you can say anything you want as long as the people running for re-election agree with you.

Here's an irony: Did you know our Pledge of Allegiance was written by a devout socialist? Francis Bellamy was a staff writer for a children's magazine. But his publisher was a devout capitalist and used Bellamy's composition in a campaign to sell subscriptions and flags to schools all over the country.

It takes courage to put your career or your student transcript on the line ... a lot more courage than yelling at your TV. Furthermore, the Bill of Rights wasn't written for the privileged, it was written to protect those more likely to be oppressed by people of privilege. It seems, though, that these iron-clad freedoms may be rusting as today's rich and powerful roll up the Constitution and use it to try to beat the marginalized back into submission.

20180927

Vipaka

You've heard the idiom about karma. Turns out, we need to brush up on our Buddhism. To correctly consider the idea, we must understand karma is more of a cause or intention with "vipaka" being the effect.

If Christian writings had indeed reached India by the 6th Century, perhaps Gautama Buddha meditated on Paul's Galatian letter and the idea of reaping what we sow. After all, Paul had borrowed the wisdom from one of his OT ancestors. But neither Paul nor Buddha compared the effects of our bad actions to what we often call a confident, strong-willed woman.

Our intention is to have a society full of functional, productive people, but in every direction, we find those who have fallen through the cracks. And so if the effect of our wishful thinking is so many dysfunctional, unproductive members of society, what are we doing wrong?

Wishing might be something for us to reconsider. We take spells of doing great things as a society, but so often we fall into the wishing well. "I wish churches would step up and help more people." "Why are charities and civic groups not doing more to help folks affected by tragedy?" "I sure do wish the homeless would straighten up and get their acts together!"

We've had our shining moments as a nation, but this is not one of them. The shine is off the apple and the core has every intention of eliminating what's left of social services. Churches and other benevolent organizations are doing all they can, but their capacity is overwhelmed already.

There is no physical force on this earth greater than an intentional nation. But make no mistake, when the intention is devoid of compassion, the vipaka is usually death and destruction.

So, as we reconsider who we are as a nation, what can each of us do in the meantime? One thing. Pick one thing. And if you're not sure what that one thing might be, consider BlueMonarch.org. This is a group which helps women and their children escape tragic circumstance. Confidence has never been in their vocabulary during their trek from the frying pan into the fire. But Blue Monarch helps them find it along with the other tools they need to lead functional, productive lives.

If your intention is to do something helpful, something positive, something life-changing, Blue Monarch is one great opportunity.

20180924

To Be an Answer to Prayer

I watched a clip recently of Arlo Guthrie singing Amazing Grace. For twelve minutes he keeps playing the melody while he talks about this and that, then sings one verse of the song. But during that rambling, he shared a sage observation from his old friend, Pete Seeger:

"If the world was perfect and everybody had money and nobody was homeless and nobody ever got sick and everybody was happy all the time, you'd have to go an awful long way out of your way to make a difference in this world. You'd have to do a whole helluva lot to try to improve the way things were. But in a world that sucks, you don't have to do very much at all."

Don't you just hate Commie bastards? Especially when their wit and wisdom so deftly shoots holes in the Randian mantra that you can't save the world, so just save yourself and take all you can get while you're at it.

It is hard to find spare time to help your neighbor. With wages stagnant for most Americans who are working longer and harder just to stay even, there's not a lot of flexibility for graciousness and mercy. But the truth is, if you don't have a lot, give a little; it goes farther than you think. One person, one meal they don't have to go without; it may not seem like much in the doing, but the person who is warmed and filled probably feels differently. It may feel to them as if they have brushed up against an angel's wing.

To be an answer to a prayer; who can aspire to be more than that?

20180915

Before the House Burns Down

Before the advent of circuit breakers, there was the fuse box. Fuses were like circuit breakers except that you had to replace them anytime you overloaded a circuit rather than just resetting the breaker.

A not uncommon way back in the day when not-so-bright folks wanted to save on fuses and keep running too many lamps or other electric things on one circuit was to put a penny behind the fuse. For just one cent they didn't have to spend any more money replacing fuses. And that worked great ... til the house burned down.

Back in the happy days when everybody liked Ike, we didn't try to provide 200-amp government services off a single 20-amp circuit. We had enough sense then to tax people and corporations based on how well they were doing in the greatest economy in the world. And it worked. We built an interstate system that way and a whole lot more. And before you launch into lamentations about interstates, imagine what it would be like today if all we had were poorly paved two-lane roads.

Pick your favorite resentment: Medicaid, food stamps, public television, whatever it may be; cut them all out completely and we'll still have mounting deficits. We need to rewire this house, not turn out the lights for the least of these. And the well-lit banquet halls should stop forwarding their electric bills to the middle-class breakfast nooks across America.

The plundering of our economic powerhouse by the privileged few must be stopped, and their functionaries sent packing ... before our house burns down.

20180913

Plutocracy

Polarize the political structure.
Plunder the social security system.
Privatize public education.
Profiteer every facet of health.
Provoke all diversity.
Prevaricate faith communities.
Profane social justice.
Praise avarice.
Proscribe scrutiny.
Paralyze reasonable discourse.

Presto … the middle class vanishes, and democracy is history.

Plutocracy with lordes and castles is formulated on the vast majority of the populace in serfdom.

Pray tell, where did you think we are heading?

20180910

Polishing Halos

The brass ring. The one we're taught to reach for. Even those far from the merry-go-round of opportunity still dream of it. And we who are more fortunate have been raised to help others who are less so.

But that was yesteryear. Now compassion is become a sign of weakness and we are all too quick to shake off Sunday School fantasy in favor of reality. Safety nets have ruined us. The corners of our fields cannot be squandered any longer. Sin is not arrogance and prosperous ease; those are evidences of success.

On the other hand, maybe what once was still is true, but the alternative facts of late are leading us down the path of our own least resistance. Perhaps the poor are not the enemy of the rich. Maybe we shouldn't kill the messengers of social justice just yet.

Though few of us ascend to positions of power, each of us helps define that power by what we are willing to accept. Autocracy occurs, not because someone up the ladder deems it so, but because of the deafening silence of each one of us below.

And this brings me to a thought that correlates clearly enough to me, but may be obtuse to anyone else of sounder mind:

If you are looking forward to eternity, you will have missed it. I'm not sure if this is something I have heard or just something I have come to believe. But the idea has been tapping more intently on the window of my consciousness lately.

If we consider the ultimate brass ring of bliss, do we truly seek to leave the troubles of this world to those who survive us and merely hope they see better days? Better days are rarely the result of wishful thinking. Strike rarely; insert never.

The point is, only in the present moment can we do anything. There is no unringing of bells. There is no lecturing the future. There is only to do today … or not to do.

The question: do we spend our time trying to polish the halos just beyond our grasp, or do we stand up and speak out for the safety and well-being of our neighbors, now and forever?

20180901

The Hemiparasitics at the Top

Wealth does not come from how hard you work. Your effort factored by your wage equals what you earn. You use X amount of infrastructure to get to and perform your work. You pay X amount of taxes to help provide the infrastructure our economic system needs to make our work and our earnings possible. But wealth results from the multiplied efforts of others; it is very rarely the result of your singular effort. When someone tells you a progressive tax system is unfair, they are being disingenuous because they are comparing an apple to an orchard.

The income of those at the top has grown exponentially over the last forty years (while working class wages have remained flat relative to the CPI). If the taxes paid by those at the top had tracked that roaring income over those forty years, there wouldn't be a spiraling federal deficit, there wouldn't be crumbling infrastructure, there wouldn't be millions of indentured college graduates struggling to keep from drowning in student loan debt ... and the list goes on.

Gordon Gekko and Ayn Rand were seductively accurate that greed is good, but they weren't right. Those at the top can expropriate a larger and larger share and have a really good time for a while, but only for as long as the system can sustain the drain. Even towering trees can eventually succumb to mistletoe (those hemiparasitic plants way up in the branches above) ... and when bridges begin falling into rivers across this country, it will probably be too late to save the mighty oak that once was our powerfully productive middle class.

20180804

One Issue

One issue. The most polarizing issue facing the electorate today. Many many people who sincerely care about starving children, the endangered environment, monstrous economic disparity, racism, the military industrial complex, the prison industrial complex, drug addiction, gerrymandering, public education, financial regulation … the list goes on and on … are setting all of these interests aside over one issue: Abortion.

That is conviction. You might even say it is the agape (self-sacrificing) love found in New Testament scripture. But it just might be that the passionate, well-intended Pro-Life movement is fiddling while Rome burns. Please at least finish reading this before you condemn me to hell, if you are not among those who already have … and even if you are, please hear me out.

The objective is to prevent all abortions. Noble. Impossible.

This end will never be achieved and even the most ardent Pro-Lifers know in their hearts that is true. Abortion law may be a single-party phenomenon, but abortions are not. The factors contributing to it run the gamut and cross all party, economic, social, racial and religious lines. It has happened throughout history. It happened before Roe v Wade. It will happen when Roe v Wade is repealed. If you pass laws making anyone who has an abortion guilty of first-degree murder, it will still happen.

You've probably heard the story of the father and daughter walking on the seashore one evening after a storm. They came across thousands of starfish that had been swept onto the beach. The little girl begins to pick them up and throw them back into the water where they could survive. The father said, "You can't save all these starfish, there are too many." She picked another up, threw it in the water and said, "I saved that one."

If the resources presently spent by the Pro-Life movement were focused on alternatives to abortion (contraception, etc) rather than outlawing abortion, the number of abortions would be dramatically reduced, the polarization would all but vanish, and all the energies presently spent by the two sides bitterly battling each other could be focused on a host of other compassionate causes … such as starving children.

Idealistic futility would be converted into overwhelming success and we wouldn't have to hate each other anymore … at least over this issue.

In the meantime, Rome is burning.

20180714

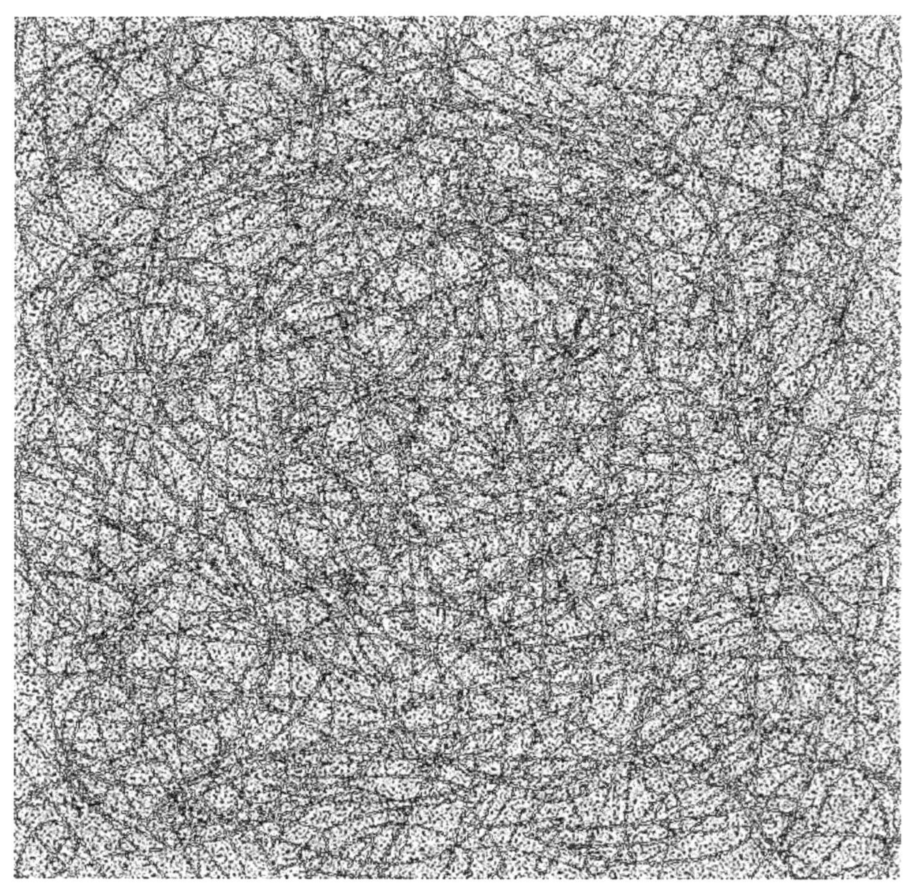

Chaos

I once worked with someone who loved chaos. He was a mechanical savant, but allergic to rules; hated not being able to do everything his way. Unfortunately, upper management was convinced they should have a say in the way his department was run. And so the game was on.

This someone figured out that his long-distance boss was prone to making exceptions to the rules when deadlines were looming, and orders would be late under the standard operating procedure. So by scheduling jobs too tightly, or under-staffing a shift, or needing to make an "emergency" repair, or, or, or … he was able to have the rules suspended … at will.

He reveled in his cleverness. But he was too clever by half.

Chaos can be exciting. Even liberating. Unless you're the one picking up the tab. Because chaos is very expensive … and destructive … even dangerous. Rules aren't much fun. But they aren't designed to be. Rules are there for protection; the operator of a machine, the society that drinks water and breathes air, the people with money in the bank, the buyers of goods and services.

Sooner or later, chaos will sink the ship.

It's possible to bail for a while … but our arms are bound to tire out.

20180706

Introspection

Abraham Lincoln may (or may not) have said, "You can fool all the people some of the time and some of the people all of the time, but you can't fool all the people all the time." Sounds like the wit and wisdom of our 16th president, and certainly true enough. How witty you find it may have something to do with where the political pendulum is and how happy you are with its direction.

James Thurber, journalist, playwright, cartoonist and author, most known for The Secret Life of Walter Mitty, did say, "You can fool too many of the people too much of the time."

But my favorite quote from Thurber: "All human beings should try to learn before they die what they are running from, and to, and why."

A bit of introspection which can, and has, and will return much value for all who consider it.

20180705

ONE WAY
ONE WAY

Dichotomy

A word we inherited from the cradle of Western culture and democracy. Two parts, divided. A word that may best describe our country. Dichotomy.

And the technique most often employed to polarize us so deeply today?

False dichotomy. Two things paired incorrectly; to deceptively claim that something must be either this or that, mutually exclusive.

For instance: "We should be worried about the hundreds of thousands of U.S. children in poverty, but we're supposed to be worried about a bunch of illegal immigrant children?!"

Civil discourse is evaporating because baseless opinion, however shameless, is being allowed to suck all the air out of the room while facts suffocate. Alternative facts are the new pronouns, relegating their verbs to indentured servitude, predicating an endless parade of perjury.

The homeless in our country are a singular catastrophe, no matter how you try to rend them. They are lost in the society which once attempted to do great things for "the least of these," but now worships at the feet of billionaire gods. If that's not a clear enough dichotomy, try this one:

Patriotism has an honorable place. Ethno-nationalism is destroying our soul.

20180626

What Would You Do?

Imagine your child has been suffering from a mysterious illness for quite some time. You've been to numerous doctors and every conceivable test has been run, but with each passing day the lack of a diagnosis is clearly a growing threat. Then finally a test comes back that explains the problem. But the report is frightening. The condition is life-threatening. The good news, though, is that a cure is available.

You wipe the tears from your eyes and ask the doctor what needs to be done. The doctor replies … "I'm thinking of a number between 1 and 100. Guess correctly and I'll tell you."

And that is how it feels to be the parent of a child in one of the dangerous regions south of our border. You've done everything you can to keep your family safe. You've tried every legal means to immigrate to a better place where people teach their children to sing about a Savior who loves all the little children in the world. You pray for a chance. But no dice.

What would you do?

A Samaritan sees a man beaten and left for dead on the road to Jericho.

He comes up to him, leans down and says, "I'm thinking of a number …"

20180625

Proof Texting

In 1551 French printer Robert Estienne published the first Bible divided into verses. His good intention was to simplify Bible study. A couple of centuries later Scottish poet Robert Burns wrote, "The best laid plans of mice and men oft go awry. What do these two things have in common?

Proof texting.

To benefit from scripture, one cannot forsake context. Without under-standing the full story or event being told, any collection of shanghaied sentences thrown together resemble a pile of bricks … not a house. In fact, ironically enough, proof-texting is often more like bricks being thrown at something or someone rather than any constructive purpose.

Jesus told stories. He didn't write fortune cookies.

On this Father's Day, it occurs to me that I may never have seen more damage done by proof-texting than the heinous events this week, justified by a couple of sentences ripped from the apostle Paul's letter to Roman Christians. When children are taken from the arms of their parents and Jesus is given the credit, well, I think the road to Hell may be behind us because evidently, we have arrived.

Perhaps that is an overstatement. There have been other times when Romans 13 has been misused. And during each of those dark times people finally stood up and said, "Enough!" During one of those episodes, our leader stood on the steps of our nation's capital and appealed to "the better angels of our nature." I hope there still is such a thing.

20180617

Dammed Blessings

The doxology I have heard and sung since my earliest memories reminds us of blessings flowing.

From various pews among sundry creatures here below, the collective praise in each venue over the years has always been to the same source of those blessings, to the one above the heavenly hosts, even if the process or parlance varied a bit.

Of course, there are those who don't believe in blessings from above, or even the above in the divine sense. The reasons why are legion. Chief among them is the difficulty of disparity. How some receive what is prayed for while others do not. Many ponderous books have been written on this one question, yet when the beseeched blessing isn't there at that most difficult moment, scholarship soothes the wound not at all.

As the echo continues to grow in houses of worship near and far, believers might do well to argue less about the accuracy of praise and do more to bust the dams we've built, inadvertently or not, that may be hindering the flow of blessings to those most in need of aid and comfort. Is it possible what we have here is a failure to be incarnate?

The "I Am" passages in the Old and New Testaments give us a clue that our faith was never meant to be a collection of passive platitudes, but rather lived out in the active voice. And since we are not the "I Am," then who and what are we to be? We are to be the hands and feet of Christ.

Resources abound. They are the blessings of God to creation. But the flow is quite another matter. And like the Dead Sea, as long as we allow our society to dam them up rather than share them all the way downstream ... so shall we be.

20180414

An Evolving Atticus

Harper Lee is upset with Aaron Sorkin. Well, not exactly. The attorney for Lee's estate is making yet another fuss about something to do with the Pulitzer prize-winning author's legacy. *To Kill A Mockingbird* is headed to Broadway, with Sorkin writing the adaptation and Jeff Daniels playing Atticus. Ironic that it is tied up in court at the moment.

You may recall a couple of years back when a second book by Lee was published; Go Set A Watchman. There have been conflicting stories about that manuscript, but the biggest issue was encountering a flawed Atticus. The prevailing opinion is that Watchman was an early draft and Mockingbird was the story Lee was most satisfied with. For years she maintained the latter would be the only book she would publish.

What Sorkin has done is make Atticus an emerging character in the play rather than the picture of perfection we watched Gregory Peck personify.

It is a brilliant adaptation of Lee's work with trademark Sorkin touches. An evolving Atticus will not only be compelling to see; it will also be good medicine for today's polarized culture. Not many of us have the courage of Lord Cromwell to be portrayed "warts and all" on canvas or otherwise. We want our best self-seen exclusively. And in this MSNBC/Fox News age, we also want to hear only what we agree with on any and every subject ... exclusively.

Sorkin is the writer and sometimes producer and/or director of such works as A Few Good Men, The West Wing, Moneyball, The Newsroom, and much more. He has a gift for giving his viewers a better appreciation of introspection. If ever there was a time when all of us could benefit from a master class in this practice, I believe it is now.

None of us have always been nor always are our best selves. Many of us have profited from mentoring and hopefully many have even been fortunate enough to experience and treasure reverse mentoring (when your children teach you things).

Since high school Atticus Finch has been one of my paragons. But an evolving Atticus, one who slowly comes to recognize his flaws and find the path to a better self ... what a role model that would be.

20180316

Doing Something!

"It won't solve the problem."

Any suggestion made regarding the epidemic of mass murders across the country is repeatedly met with this response. But even though no pill cures all illness, pharmacies abound.

Speaking of ill, aren't you sick of hearing the "won't solve the problem" artifice yet? I haven't heard it come off the lips of one person not smart enough to understand that it is disingenuous at best. They surely don't bother to contemplate just how pernicious it is to be among those categorically opposing any efforts to reduce this slaughter.

The next time you hug your grandchild, think about this. If banning bump stocks (or instituting better background checks, closing the gun show loophole, et al ... take your pick) only saved one person this year, what if your arms are wrapped around that person? Or what if tomorrow it is you who never gets that chance again with one of your loved ones, like so many other grieving families?

Dick's Sporting Goods didn't solve the problem this week. But they did something. The kids standing up and speaking out in Parkland haven't solved the problem. But they are doing something. More and more, people have had all they're going to take ... and they are doing something!

Come senators, congressmen
Please heed the call
Don't stand in the doorway
Don't block up the hall
For he that gets hurt
Will be he who has stalled
There's a battle outside
And it is ragin'.
It'll soon shake your windows
And rattle your walls
For the times they are a-changin'.

20180228

THE
GILDED
AGE
A TALE OF TO DAY.

Gilded

"Thoughts and prayers …" Once a phrase offering comfort, now so politically polluted you hesitate to speak it for fear of being heard to say, "life is tough and there's nothing you can do about it."

Once upon a time our society could and did effect change when crises arose. We prayed. Then we put feet on our prayers and stood up to profiteers whose pockets bulged with bloody money. Today we could, but sadly often don't. And so nothing changes … except the dissolution of democracy as we once knew it.

We passively watch as a new gilded age takes shape. A generation from now our environment may be unrecognizable, our schools may seem more like prisons (the least we can do). But on the bright side, perhaps a penitent plutocrat or two will build a few libraries.

20180217

Ballistic Trauma

Dear Next Church or School or Public Venue,

Our thoughts and prayers will be with you when dozens or scores or hundreds of your group die in the next hideous hail of bullets. We hope you know our nation will be grieving for you. We will be truly sorry. But you must understand, this country has collectively decided that you are expendable. You will be what is sometimes referred to as "acceptable losses." Taking any steps to control or regulate the means by which you will be killed could be depicted as an impingement on freedom, and so your American neighbors (that is, your North American neighbors (that is, your U.S. neighbors)) have conceded the necessity that you pay the price.

Thank you for your sacrifice.

Although you might be heartened by statistics you may hear of other countries (virtually every other developed country in the world) where tenable controls have led to phenomenal reductions in munition-induced mortality, any hope that our Congress will consider such details or measures is sadly misguided. The votes are firmly in place to maintain the status quid-pro-quo (and they and those who quid them have ever-growing security available to ensure they don't share your impending fate).

After all, new regulations won't change anything if our government doesn't bother to follow the rules on the books. And if the prevalent attitude allows for the disregard of any protections in place, you can see how inevitable ballistic trauma is in your future … or at least someone you know.

The dismal truth is, we have evolved beyond survival of the fittest to a new paradigm, and neither you nor I have the funds to get into that paradigm.

P.S. - While we can't buy our way out of this problem, we might vote our way to safety, if we live long enough.

20171107

The Other Side of Heaven

A childhood memory has been bouncing around in my head the past few days. I think it was shortly after the death of a close relative. The lady who stayed with us in the afternoons while my mom was working said to me that it was sad to lose someone close, but we would all get to be together in heaven again someday.

Being a curious grade schooler, I thought about it and then asked her if there were two sides of heaven.

Let me digress for a minute. As far back as I can remember, there was always something going on where my dad had to go take a picture for the paper. City meetings. Social gatherings. Service projects. And I often got to tag along. No doubt I'd met more businessmen, politicians and civic leaders than any other kid in town. I'd even been in the upstairs of the Masonic lodge... both of them.

When he wasn't out taking pictures, Dad was usually at his light table in the print shop, cutting film together so plates could be burned, and jobs printed. No telling how many important hands I got to shake by that light table when I was there after school or in the summertime. Dad had a desk, but he never used it. He was on the shop floor almost all the time. If you came to see him, Miss Alma ushered you back. I think part of the message was that he didn't mind stopping what he was doing for a moment to talk ... and the other part of the message was to notice the work that needed not to be neglected too long.

A host of folks came in that shop. Often smiling. Sometimes not. But the takeaway for me was the way they were always treated with respect. Whether they were mad or not. Whether they were big shots or not. And whether they lived on 5th Street or 1st Street. If I was standing there, I was supposed to shake hands and say "sir." Wasn't taught any different. Didn't know any different.

So back to the two sides of heaven. You put the pieces of a puzzle together a little at a time. All God's children go to heaven. But a child notices that the black people all live on one side of town, the whites on the other. It was a reasonable question. Her answer, wise and understanding. "There aren't white people and black people in heaven, just people, all thankful just to be with God."

It has taken me a long time to understand my reaction. I told her it wasn't true ... through angry tears. She was wrong. I knew because I had an illustrated Child's Bible Story Book. There was a picture of Jesus in it ... and he was white.

I wasn't upset at the idea there were black people in heaven ... or whether there were two sides of heaven. But even a small child who has been taught to respect all people still sees how the world is, and it was a terrifying prospect for a child in the 60s that someday I might not get to be white anymore.

We've come a long way in this country since then. We've put the sheets away, mostly. And we don't have to call it "Bombingham" anymore. But we're not color-blind yet, and sadly the same fear still lingers in some hearts that I faced that day as a child. From experience let me say, it can cause a person to say and do very stupid things. May we hasten the day, on this side of heaven, when there aren't white people and black people anymore, just people, all thankful just to be with God ... and each other.

20170516

Volunteerism

Why do people volunteer? More specifically, what causes people to spend time working without pay? It is complicated, yet simple. There are all kinds of reasons why, yet the result is almost always the same: to help others.

The results of volunteerism are usually tangible and measurable. The catalyst, however, is often harder to identify and define; and while essential to the formula, it is all but impossible to manufacture or package. You don't hire volunteers, you inspire them.

It is not a simple thing to inspire people to suspend attention to the demands on their time and money to offer their energies without pay. But discourage them by compromising the results of their unselfish efforts and inspiration will surely disappear like mist in the morning sun.

The National Cornbread Festival is an organization comprised of and completely dependent on volunteers. In its 21-year history, it has provided funds to a wide variety of groups, projects and causes. And beyond the substantial infusion of cash, it has also generated a spirit of cooperation envied by numerous festival planners near and far who have visited this community to learn the "secrets" that have led to so much success.

There have been many obstacles over the years and more than a few missteps, as with any human institution. But each setback has been met with a steadfast resolve to work through the difficulties, knowing that the benefit to the community is well worth the effort.

What is "community?" Is it a municipal entity or is it more than that? The National Cornbread Festival is a community event that takes place in the City of South Pittsburg. What does the city "get out of it?" This community gets every cent. Cornbread money has helped restore landmarks, bought mountains of school supplies and equipment, repainted and rewired churches, sponsored field trips for students and senior citizens, covered boys and girls scouts camp fees, bought athletic equipment, and the list goes on and on. Some of that money was local, but most of it came out of the pockets of visitors from all over the country.

Cornbread volunteers do what they do for love of community. What would happen if an effort was made to co-opt them as unpaid municipal staff? Would hundreds and hundreds still show up to work their butts off? Probably not. And South Pittsburg would be a BIG loser. The inspiration would be gone ... and the money with it.

Does South Pittsburg belong to its city government or is it the other way around. The City of South Pittsburg has always been a vital part of the National Cornbread Festival. Hopefully that is allowed to continue for many years to come.

20170509

The Johnson Amendment

In the mid-1950s, Senator Lyndon Johnson was able to get a provision added to the IRS Code which prohibited 501(c)(3) organizations from supporting or opposing political candidates. The intent was not to abridge free speech, but to prevent special interests from abusing the tax-exempt status of churches and other non-profit groups.

The "Johnson amendment" has never prevented pastors from speaking out on issues. And there is a great deal of evidence that it has done little to restrain endorsements or the inverse action. Consider the fact it was added several years before more than a few Protestant pulpits raged against the candidacy of "papist" John F. Kennedy for president.

This provision has served, however, to quarantine churches from the plague of campaign finance fever, or to use another metaphor, keep the moneychangers outside the temple gates. Any serious attempt to eliminate this hedge between politics and religion will surely pierce us through with many sorrows.

Granted, if this breach were allowed, most churches would likely not purpose to become SuperPAC cash boxes. But those that didn't would still find it much harder to escape the broad brush of skepticism that has already been emptying pews for at least a generation.

Cambering libel laws to subdue journalists from reporting unflattering facts would weaken our democracy. Laundering campaign contributions through our churches would oxidize our faith.

20170504

The Foolishness of Sunday School?

Some seem determined to repurpose our society, eradicating safety nets in order to commandeer more money for the military ... not veteran's benefits, mind you, but a weapons stockpile already higher than the rest of the world combined.

As Christians head into Holy Week and follow the story in the latter parts of the gospels, one passage seems to pulsate with regard to the dispositional parallels. The powers that be were fed up with the "love your neighbor" movement and were taking steps to cross it off the landscape. The apostles' reaction was the sword. Jesus' response to them, "That is enough." He probably wasn't talking about the number of swords they had or could obtain. More likely he was speaking to the way they were inclining altogether.

This begs the question for us. How are we inclining? Have we become fed up with the sacrifices necessary to take care of the sick and poor among us? Have we concluded that the sermon on the mount was fanciful foolishness which may be fine for Sunday School but useless in the real world?

Our words don't answer these questions. Our actions do. The heart of the matter, regardless of what we say, is where we put our treasure.

20170406

KIMBERLY

Dedication

I've bought one really nice piece of jewelry in my life. You can wager a guess as to what and for whom. There is a proverb that says her price is far above rubies. I'm not sure about that because I've never tried to sell her. But all who have crossed our path over the years have appraised justly for me that is perhaps a modest estimation. Even though she has never fooled with flax, never bought a field, never planted a vineyard ... I can't count all the times I have seen her extend a helping hand to those in need. But she doesn't wear silk, rarely wears purple (except when our kids were at Lipscomb). Maybe a New Testament scripture might be helpful here.

"Whatsoever things are true, whatsoever things are honest, whatsoever things are just, whatsoever things are pure, whatsoever things are lovely, whatsoever things are of good report; if there be any virtue, if there be any praise ..."

I have thought on these things about her all our years together,

but appreciating them out loud I've done not nearly enough.

www.ingramcontent.com/pod-product-compliance
Lightning Source LLC
Chambersburg PA
CBHW071019180726
48291CB00004B/1540

* 9 7 8 1 9 4 9 8 8 8 9 7 3 *